The
Ten Principles of Respect

The Ten Principles of Respect

Published by: Anything Print
P. O. Box 28073, Sunnyside
Pretoria 0132.
South Africa

Copyright© 2018 by Elizabeth Abba Great.

ISBN: 978-0-620-45621-0

All rights reserved. Except for use in any review, the reproduction or utilization of this book in whole or in part in any form be electronic, mechanical, or other means, now known or hereafter invented, is forbidden without the written permission of the publisher:

All scriptures are taken from the King James Version of the Holy Bible except otherwise stated.

Contents

Acknowledgment	5
Dedication	7
Introduction	9
Point One: Respect is Reciprocal	13
Point Two: Respect is given before its Received	14
Point Three: Integrity is key	17
Point Four: It is about Value	19
Point Five: It is about World View	22
Point Six: It is a Product of Healthy Self-Image	24
Point Seven: Respect is Earned	26
Point Eight: It is About Knowing the Creator	28
Point Nine: Purpose Makes a Difference	30
Point Ten: Respect Attracts	33
Conclusion	**35**

Acknowledgment

Whatever I am today, I owe it to the effort of certain people who saw greatness in me early and invested to the last of their cent and time to brush me to the level.

First on the list of these people is the late Mr. L.S. Molope whose gentle soul has gone to rest in the Lord's bosom. He made sure I acquire all the necessary knowledge I need to get to where I am today.

Second is Mr Sarel Theron who gave his time tirelessly to brush me and bring the gold on the inside of me out so I can be a blessing to my generation. Thank you very much Sarel, I want to assure you that the seed you sowed in my life is about to do wonders to God be all the glory.

Thirdly my husband, Emmanuel Abba Great who saw the writing skill in me and spend his time to package my works. Thank you.

I also want to use this time to thank my long standing friends whose constant encouragement through my dark days helped me to face life again. Sadia Hanslo and family, Thank you. Irene Erasmus and Benny thank you.

To Mbali Pretty Arojojoye, the founder and director of Ark of Hope Southern Africa, a beloved daughter whose ministry has greatly refreshed me and my family.

I also want to thank my parent for assisting me by talking care of my children to have time to invest in the great projects. Thank you Mom and Dad you are the best.

I also want to thank my children for being patient with me. Thank you Michael, Clifford, Caiaphas. I love you very much God bless you.

I also want to thank my brothers, Jeremiah, Dennis lastly is my late brother Thomas, whose gentle soul has gone to rest in the Lord's bosom.

Dedication

I dedicate this book to the Almighty God without who my life would have been a waste and Jesus Christ, the author and finisher of my faith. Thank you Lord.

Introduction

Respect is about regards and how we see every other person around us. It is impossible to respect the other person if we do not believe he/she has anything to offer usually as humans.

We tend to respect those that are way ahead of us therefore disregarding and disrespecting those around us.

The height of respect is when we see each other from the point of being human, not for what that individual has or who that individual is. Our present generation is so corrupt and materialistic that the word 'respect' has lost its meaning. Society has gone wild, making the family structure which is the foundation of all to take a nose dive. Some wives do not submit to their husband, some children do not take instructions from their parents and some husband find it difficult to be faithful and loyal to their wives and to provide for the families as the bible encourages.

Respect is what we esteem, or have a sense of worth for a person or group of people, without which we stand to face the doom of its consequences, which is what we are going to look at in The Ten Principles of Respect.

The principles of respect takes its roots on the belief that every other person is human like us. Until we look at each person as creation of God with hidden potential, able to change the world if helped, we can never reap the ultimate fruit of respect.

Below, we shall be looking at the TEN PRINCIPLES OF RESPECT and how to maximize them to make a better, strong, secure and great society. Over the years, we can see how society has lost its social values for superficiality in the name of development. The sustainable development is that which adds to our value and not to destroy it.

In the African context, respect is highly rated, which is why the family value and communal lifestyle is still in existence in most of our rural areas.

In as much as scientific discoveries and development have contributed greatly to society, by giving us easy alternatives to the way we do things, they have equally contributed in destroying our social values, which has respect as its core foundation; this is why today, people can kill just for little things, rape a child and do things that once upon a time were unheard of.

How do we recapture this social values and bring sanity to our society? when all that count in our time is how much an individual has or where they work, how educated or which school they attended. The society is sick and I believe that our values needs to be addressed and recapture.

Before we look at the Ten Principles of Respect, it is important we look at what respect is not, for the sake of clarity.

In Africa, when we talk about respect, certain thoughts jump into minds, which are behind certain behaviors and cruelty that culminate to anti-social actions and crime to humanity.

- ❖ Respect is not about age
- ❖ Respect cannot be demanded
- ❖ Respect is not a ground for pride
- ❖ It is not about people bowing down to you
- ❖ It is not about your title or achievement
- ❖ It is not about who you know or where you have been.
- ❖ It is not your appearance
- ❖ Neither about how educated or rich one is
- ❖ It can never be bought
- ❖ Does not intimidate

What respect is not, will help you to appreciate and understand what respect really is; It easy to fake respect but the true respect cannot be hidden or faked. It shows in the eye, composure and in speeches and if subjected to time, it last through generations.

The outward show of respect, is not respect. The true respect reflects in jealousy from enemies and loyalty from friends and subordinates. Respect can be felt and noticed even in the midst of equals. Respect can also be seen in silence especially among the high and mighty.

With this background in mind. I believe you are better informed now to face the principles of respect.

Respect is Reciprocal

When you respect people, they respect you back. Respect is reciprocal which comes naturally without any force or coercion.

Respect obeys the law of sowing and reaping, when you sow respect, you will definitely reap respect. In this context, you receive respect from the person or people you show respect to.

It is a Give and Take and in the same measure you give it. It takes two eagle as it is commonly said therefore, respect is reciprocal.

Respect is First Given Before Received

Unlike the first point, Respect is first given before it is received. If anyone desires to be respected, let him be the first to give it out and the law of reciprocal will take effect. Respect from the point I made initially, is not about bowing down or looking timid towards those to whom you are giving the respect to, it is about regard and value. If you consider the other person as human, then you will treat them with a certain level of dignity you believe they deserve..

I came to realize that even little children are happy when they discover that you treat them with respect even though they are still young. This enable them to contribute to mature talk in confidence. When you talk to them respectfully, not joining the people that look down on them, they tend to love you and would want to tell you everything that hurts them.

Respect for people can be sown by listening to them attentively when they talk. A lot of people are emotionally strained with no one to talk to, let alone to be listened to.

They seek attention from the society, which most of the time, they do not get due to the busy nature of our society a factor affecting and plaguing our time. they end up developing low self- esteem, thinking they are being ignored and not loved. They start to regard themselves as failures, useless beings and non-achievers. This circle of event is responsible for the reduction in productivity at home, school an in the work place.

Our social fabrics are breaking by the day because people are not respecting the feelings of one another. If we cannot even listen to each other, give words of encouragement when we can, and offer help with the little we can, then how can our world become a better place.

It is important to note that everyone is important in his or her own way. Everyone is contributing something to the world in one way or the other. Therefore we need to respect everyone we meet whether rich or poor, white or black, irrespective of gender, religion and belief. it is also important to remember, we are first humans before we were divided along racial and religious lines - a man made difference established to destroy the plans of God.

Integrity is Key

Integrity is self-respect. Respect comes to those that respect themselves. When a man respects him or herself, it shows in the way he or she speaks, composes him or herself, and behaves even where there is no one to see him or her. Self-respect is about self-discovery and self-value. If we respect ourselves, certain things we do for material gain will not be done.

Everyday in the news we hear about people who cast away their garment of respect, indulging in shameful acts that are void of respect. We read stories of corruption among the high and mighty in our society. People that should be looked up to, to make quality decision on behalf of the nation, engage in shameful acts simply because of lack of integrity.

Integrity is a virtue that cannot be bought but cultivated through self–discipline. When we think of people of integrity, we cannot but mention legends like Nelson Mandela, a man who fought for the freedom of his people and was not interested in position of power. He showed his integrity by the way he ruled and handed over power, when others should be fighting to keep it for themselves.

If there is any virtue our society need above every other today, is that of integrity keeping our words not promising people heaven and earth for the purpose of getting what we want and then turn our backs on them later. There is no other virtue that attracts respect from the high and mighty, poor and downtrodden like integrity.

Wherever we are, in whatever position we find ourselves, it is important to note that integrity is one priceless virtue that can take us to any height and keep us there: it is equally important to note that integrity will make you more enemies if you desire to have this priceless virtue. Integrity ensures the truth prevails and justice is done against the unjust in favour of the just irrespective of their statues in the society.

It is About Value

Respect is about what we place value on. Some have their value in themselves, having all the best for themselves while others have their value in a better society devoid of corruption and social ills and so on. People's value differs making us creatures of value, we tend to run towards certain values and away from others. What we value, we respect and hold in high regard.

Our energy and passion are driven daily towards our values. This can be ascertained in what an individual spends his/ her money on. To those whose value is centered on looking good, they can spend to the last cent on clothes and make ups; while those whose value is centered on people can use their money and energy to help and uplift humanity.

If we want to change what we respect it is very important we change our values in line with what we desire to respect. If we want to respect people and be respected, which is the core of this write up, then we need to shift our values to people. People who have discovered the secret of greatness are reaping from this secret.

Those that are poor and struggling are those that set their values on meaningless and mundane things. Life is about value, men who become great achieve their dreams because they set their values on great things, because that is what attracts respect.

If we value ourselves, then we will respect one another, which will help to recapture our societal values that are fast eroding.

If we only value money material things, which is the direction our world is fast heading, then our society will continue to deteriorate because money is not meant to be an end but a means to an end. When we make money but lack human value, we will use the same money to look for cure for the consequences of the value we lacked. The reason people are abusing substances daily is because they have put money and material things above human value and when that is realized, they suddenly realize that life is more than the acquisition wealth and material things; so in search of meaning, they begin to experiment on substances.

The cure of these ills is enshrined in the recapture of respect as it has always been known in the African culture as 'UBUNTU'.

It is About World View

World view is about the way we see our world in relation to the world around us. Decisions are made based on world view; likewise we make progress in life based on the same.

We respect our world view than that of others until we meet with people who seemed to know more than we do. Respect is based on world view and as we expand our world view, we begin to respect others and their opinion, if not, we are going to stick to our small world, thinking we are sufficient in ourselves.

Our world view, helps us to be humble and receive other people with love knowing that we are a member of one big family called the human race. the most hardened people are those with narrow world view.

We came with nothing into the world and would certainly take nothing out, therefore, whatever we acquire, would certainly be left behind. with that knowledge behind our minds, we should conduct ourselves in manners that is worthy of respect.

The less people know, the more proud they are. I quite understand that knowledge puffs up, but when knowledge is pushed at a certain level, it results in humility. A wise man once said," I know enough to know that I know nothing yet which is worth knowing" That means, the more you know; the more there is to know. When we get to the level in life where we begin to see from a different perspective, then respect for all we see comes naturally.

It Is A Product of Healthy Self- Image.

To respect others without the fear of losing neither face, nor intimidated by the other person's status of what they have acquired, shows a healthy self – image. Self-image is simply the way an individual sees themselves.

Do you think someone else is better than you because they are more educated, richer, sophisticated etc.? To have true respect for people, a healthy self-image is necessary without which people get jealousy and envious.

This is one of the monster that is plaguing our society today; because people major themselves and value themselves by themselves, crime becomes the issue of the day, people killing one another through poison, assassinations and all forms of devious ways.

If we truly believe in ourselves, we will develop a healthy self image that will make us to value ourselves in whatever level we find ourselves in the society.

Respect is Earned

From the few points elaborated above, it can be deduced that respect is earned. It cannot be bought or imposed on. No matter how rich an individual is, his or her wealth will not be able to earn him or her respect; unless he or she used it to serve humanity.

Under this point, we shall look at the character of an individual as a yardstick for true and genuine respect. I have realized that if a child of ten years of age behave himself, saying the right words at the right time and with a quality of character that goes with it, that child would be more respected than a man as old as Methuselah or as rich as King Solomon without such quality of character.

Character makes a person. When people describe an individual, they usually use the person's character, which means character is what earns anyone respect and his or her possessions.

It is about Knowing the Creator

Everyone to some extend believe there is a creator somewhere who created the world. This is why humans are religious, because there is an inner instinct that agrees with every human being that there is supreme being that created this world and the people in it.

The Holy Bible puts it in this way, God created man in His image and after His likeness'. If this statement is true which I believe it is, then every human being is God's incarnate and carried God's DNA running in him or her. If we have this understanding, then we will consider everybody we meet as God's offspring irrespective of status, color, race or creed.
The creator does not discriminate neither favors a certain class of people above the other but gives

freely to all, which is a sign of regard and honor. It is written in the book of Psalms 8:3-4

> *"When I consider the heavens, the works of your fingers, the moon and the stars which thou has ordained.*
>
> *What is man you are so mindful of him? And the son of man that thou visited him?"*

If God will so consider man and value him, how much more we His creatures ought to value and regard each other.

Purpose Makes A Different

Everyone of us are specially packaged for a particular purpose, which most often is not known to anyone around us or to us, unless we take time to find out.

Purpose is where the secret of everyone's success is hidden and no two people's purpose are the same. The Wright Brothers were purposed to discover aero dynamism without them, we probably would still be without planes, talk less of jets and rockets.

Thomas Edison was purposed to discover electricity and he answered the call of purpose; to bless the world with electricity; without which the world would be completely shot down in darkness. I would lack the space to write about men like Michael

Faraday, Newton etc. Men that were without repute from obscure background; that listened to the call of purpose to do things that the whole world cannot do without, for generation to come.

The same qualities are locked up in each and everyone person that made up the seven billion population of the earth today, but because we fail to see these great wealth in an individual, we lack the ability to regard and respect them; giving them the reason not to value themselves, therefore, locking up the potentials within them, depriving ourselves the profit that could have been realized to the betterment of humanity.

If we can believe in people, respect their views no matter how foolish they sound, we can help the vast majority of unmotivated individual to appreciate themselves, therefore bringing out the best in them to make the world a better place.

I imagine what the contribution of every individual would make to the world, when some are singing songs, others are writing books, while others are manufacturing big machines. This is to show that the world has not seen anything yet.

There is more wealth hidden in an individual than there in the gulf of Iraq and the gold mine of South Africa put together. Let us value one another and help each other to bring out the best in them.

Respect Attracts

Respect attracts respect. The law of attraction comes into place when we give out respect. People are attracted to those that respect them irrespective of their position and status.

Everyone wants to be respected. If we can take advantage of this, then we will find ourselves with the high and mighty.

When people are attracted to you, it also bring with it favour. there is so much of poverty among people today because respect is not valued. respect draws the best out of people to those that gives it. when as a student, you respect your teacher, he or she will definitely give his or her best to you. same with parents, elders, government officials and everyday people.

Today, neighbours can live together just with a brick wall separating them, yet knows next to nothing about each other, when it is possible the he or she might be the person in possession of the key to your next level.

Human beings are creatures of relationships, therefore to overlook the law of respect is to subject oneself to self imprisonment and slow death.

Conclusion

What you give you attract; what you value, you respect and what you respect comes to you.
Do you want to have quality people in your life? Then respect the presence of people and you will have them come to your life.

The principles of respect is to see others as one of us not one of them. The greatest enemy of the 21st century is identity crisis, people want to belong, which is the reason for cliques and all kinds of social groups.

The principle of respects if followed, will make our world a wonderful place to dwell in.

I am a South African woman and I weep every time I

see the way our society is gradually degenerating because this very virtue is not given attention to. I watch with tears, learners in high school beating their teachers, stabbing them to death, clearly showing the absence of respect.

Crime is on a daily increase with nothing the government can do about it scaring away investors and those that could salvage our economy from total collapse.

I have therefore joined the president of the Republic to say "THUMA MINA" send me to make a difference so that we can save our country, our continent Africa and our world by restoring respect back to our families, schools, government and our society in general.

Let us follow the points outlined here and watch our generation transformed to what it is supposed to be, where value will lead.

Other Books by Elizabeth

1. The Journey of my life with Jesus Christ

2. God Heals

3. Anointing that breaks the yokes

4. The Holy Communion

5. Praying according to the will of God

6. Evil Altars

7. Thuma Mina (Novel)

www.ingramcontent.com/pod-product-compliance
Lightning Source LLC
Chambersburg PA
CBHW031508040426
42444CB00007B/1259